CONTENTS

INTRODUCTION

"One person's terrorist is another person's freedom fighter." This phrase has been used so often, it has become a cliché. In the world of terrorism and counterterrorism, the ideas of right versus wrong and good versus evil are gray and murky. But they are especially unclear when discussing an armed group dedicated to liberating a homeland for its people.

Supporters of national liberation causes have argued that terrorism is an equalizing force. It has permitted the have-nots to battle the haves and to sound their cries for freedom to an international court of opinion. People who are poor, outnumbered, and without a political voice have often seen their nationalistic hopes quashed. National aspirations left unanswered traditionally have resulted in desperation. Desperation usually has led to violence. Yet at what point do the ends justify the means in the search for statehood?

Many of the seemingly irreconcilable nationalistic conflicts of our times have turned into terrorist struggles. Supporters of the Irish Republic Army (IRA) have justified centuries of conflict by using the argument that the divided island nation of Ireland must be united. Supporters of the campaign to end British rule of Northern Ireland have argued that terrorist attacks against the British military, against the local police, and even against civilians are justified.

Basque terrorists in Spain have long waged a campaign against the Spanish government to set up an independent Basque state that would preserve the unique Basque culture and language. Cleverly staged bombings and high-profile assassinations throughout Spain have targeted police officers and politicians.

The Kurds of southwestern Asia are surrounded by some of the world's most unforgiving political and geographical landscapes. They, too, have justified the use of terrorism against the Turks, the Iraqis, and the Iranians as a weapon in their age-old quest for an independent Kurdish nation.

TERRORIST DOSSIERS

AT ANY COST

National Liberation
TERRORISM

Samuel M. KATZ

Lerner Publications Company/Minneapolis

To S., Y., and M.—It's all for you.
SMK

Publishers Note: The information in this book was current at the time of publication. However, the publisher is aware that news involving current events dates quickly. Please refer to the websites on page 69 for places to go to obtain up-to-date information.

Lerner Publications Company
A division of Lerner Publishing Group
241 First Avenue North
Minneapolis, Minnesota U.S.A.

Website address: www.lernerbooks.com

Library of Congress Cataloging-in-Publication Data

Katz, Samuel M., 1963–
      At any cost: national liberation terrorism / by Samuel M. Katz.
            p.   cm. — (Terrorist dossiers)
      Summary: Describes the history and current situation of various National Liberation movements throughout the world.
      Includes bibliographical references and index.
      ISBN: 0–8225–0949–0 (lib. bdg. : alk. paper)
      1. National liberation movements—Juvenile literature. 2. Nationalism—Juvenile literature.
3. Terrorism—Juvenile literature. [1. National liberation movements. 2. Nationalism.
3. Terrorism.] I. Title. II. Series.
JC312.K38 2004
322.4'2—dc21   2002151703

Manufactured in the United States of America
1 2 3 4 5 6 – DP – 09 08 07 06 05 04

The ongoing cycle of violence between Tamil terrorists on the island of Sri Lanka and the Sinhalese government has left thousands dead and many missing. Guerrilla warfare, suicide bombings, and repeated attacks on the country's leaders have brought continued instability to the nation.

The fighting in Northern Ireland, Turkey, Spain, and Sri Lanka all involve conflicts of race or religion dating back hundreds of years. Over time, the ethnic and religious groups of these countries—some of which had lived in their territories for thousands of years—suddenly found themselves stateless, without basic civil rights, and living under what was to them foreign occupation. Powerless and desperate, they radicalized their view of the world. National liberation armies and underground guerrilla armies—many of which rely on terrorist tactics—came to be seen as the only means by which national aspirations could be promoted and eventually negotiated.

Terrorist groups have proven to be unflappable foes in battle and unflinching political forces at the negotiation table. By the violence they bring forth and by the hope they attempt to keep ablaze, they have shaped the world in which we live.

The results of a car bombing in Madrid, Spain

WHO'S WHO AND
WHAT'S WHAT

British government: operating from London, England, the authority that has sent troops to Northern Ireland and has implemented some harsh policies but that has also worked to negotiate peace

Good Friday Agreement: the 1998 peace accord that set forth power sharing among the Catholic and Protestant political parties

Irish Republican Army (IRA): Sinn Féin's military arm, no longer much of a force in Northern Ireland

Provisional IRA (PIRA): a splinter group of Sinn Féin's military arm, Northern Ireland's largest paramilitary group

Real IRA (RIRA): a splinter group of the PIRA, made up of experienced bomb makers who object to the peace negotiations

Royal Ulster Constabulary (RUC): Northern Ireland's police force, made up mostly of Protestants. Renamed the Police Service of Northern Ireland in 2001 as part of overall reform

Sinn Féin: the political wing of the PIRA. The wing's leader is Gerry Adams.

the Troubles: the name given to the ongoing cycle of violence in Northern Ireland

THE
IRISH REPUBLICAN ARMY
AND ITS
OFFSHOOTS

One of history's oldest terrorist wars—and certainly one of the world's longest-standing religious wars—is the battle over Ireland. For centuries, the Roman Catholic majority of Ireland has fought against its second-class status on the island. The Irish Catholics have struggled to gain and hold political and socioeconomic dominance over the Anglo-Irish Protestants, who form a strong minority.

HISTORICAL ROOTS
The Irish conflict's historical roots are deep, dating back to A.D. 432 and the arrival of Patrick, a Roman Catholic missionary. Patrick hailed from Great Britain and came to Ireland to convert the local people to Christianity. The Gaels inhabited Ireland at the time and followed the Druidic religion, a pagan faith.

Patrick's work was successful, and Christianity became the primary religion in Ireland. But because of the island's isolation from the rest of Europe and from the seat of the Roman Catholic Church in faraway Rome, the inhabitants combined traditional Catholic practices with local pagan traditions. The Roman Catholic pope Adrian IV wanted to purge pagan rituals from Irish practices. In 1155 he issued a decree granting Henry II, the Catholic king of England, lordship over Ireland.

Henry sent an army to subdue the Irish, and he put in place several anti-Irish laws. He banned the use of Gaelic, for example, the historic local language. He outlawed English-Irish marriages, even though at this time both groups followed the Catholic faith. Henry's policies launched centuries of English political, cultural, and economic dominance of Ireland.

7

In 1533 King Henry VIII established the Anglican Church, a move that broke England's ties to the Roman Catholic Church. The members of this new church were called Protestants. For the next 250 years, English monarchs encouraged Protestants to emigrate from Great Britain to the Irish island, especially to Ulster, a historic northeastern region made up of nine counties. These Protestant newcomers were loyal to the Protestant ruler and got Irish land cheaply. In this way, the Irish island was taken over by outsiders, and its native inhabitants became a powerless majority.

THE BATTLE OF THE BOYNE

Battles fought in Ireland hundreds of years ago remain rallying cries for generations of Catholics and Protestants. The most notable such fight was the Battle of the Boyne on July 1, 1690. It pitted the French and Irish armies of the ousted Catholic English king, James II, against English forces under their new Protestant king, William of Orange. The battle, fought on the banks of the Boyne River north of Dublin, Ireland, ended with a Protestant victory. Protestants in Ireland adopted the color orange as their symbol of superiority. Each summer they march through Catholic neighborhoods to remind their Catholic neighbors of the Protestants' epic victory and the Catholics' painful defeat. ■

The English passed a number of anti-Catholic laws that further diminished Irish culture and status. Catholics could not vote, own land, or go to college. By the late 1700s, these measures, which didn't apply to Protestants on the island, were causing turmoil and rebellion.

HOME RULE

Responding to the unrest that was erupting throughout Ireland, England formally united with Ireland, Scotland, and Wales in 1801 to form the United Kingdom of Great Britain and Ireland. One of the goals of this British Act of Union was to put Ireland more firmly under British control from the capital in London, England. In Ireland, however, especially among radical extremists and the impoverished, the act further inflamed the dream of an independent Irish nation.

In the mid-1840s, Ireland dealt with the devastation of a blight that nearly eliminated its potato crop, the country's staple food. The British government did little to alleviate the resulting famine, which caused two million deaths and motivated nearly two million Irish men, women, and children to emigrate to North America. The British government's behavior in Ireland's time of need was further proof to Catholics that British rule was destroying the Irish people.

Calls for Irish independence mounted in the late 1800s and early 1900s, as did the notion of Home Rule. This idea would allow Britain to continue to set foreign and defense policies for Ireland but would leave domestic matters in the hands of an independent Irish parliament. Ulster, where Protestants were a majority, was strongly set against Home Rule. Meanwhile, a new political party—Sinn Féin, Gaelic for "We Ourselves"—was formed to lead the fight for Irish independence.

Under pressure from Protestant unionists, who wanted to continue to be part of the United Kingdom, Britain balked at Home Rule legislation for several decades. Finally, in 1914, a bill was passed. Of the nine Ulster counties, six—Antrim, Down, Armagh, Londonderry, Tyrone, and Fermanagh—chose to remain part of the United Kingdom. The counties of Cavan, Donegal, and Monaghan chose to stand with Ireland.

Most Protestants in Ulster did not favor the idea of Home Rule. Here, police officers enter a Protestant section of Belfast, County Antrim, in the early 1900s to quiet an anti-Home Rule march that had turned violent.

(The outbreak of World War I (1914–1918) later that year postponed the bill's implementation.)

While pleased that Home Rule would eventually give them more rights, many Irish wanted more. They wanted full independence immediately in a united Ireland that included the six counties of Ulster. Sinn Féin formed the Irish Republican Brotherhood (IRB), a military force that organized the Easter Rising in 1916. This uprising pitted armed IRB members against British troops garrisoned in Dublin, the capital of Ireland.

■ ■

April 24, 1916—Easter Monday
The sight of the men carrying their arms *down the main streets in Dublin electrified the city's residents, who had long dreamed of challenging British rule. The men of the IRB's Dublin Battalion carried whatever weapons they could find—shotguns, Mauser pistols, and Lee-Enfield .308s—and a day's rations as they paraded through*

British soldiers stand amid the rubble of the General Post Office after the Easter Rising in 1916.

the city. They were determined to seize the Irish capital and to wrestle it—and the rest of the island—from British occupation. By shortly after noon, the Dublin Battalion had taken over the General Post Office, the Four Courts, three of the railway terminals, and other important points in central Dublin. These buildings were flying the tricolor of the Irish flag, not the British Union Jack. Sinn Féin leaders proudly announced the formation of an independent Irish republic.

The Easter Rising caught British forces by surprise. The following day, forty-five hundred British troops, supported by armored cars with machine guns, stormed IRB lines. The counterassault on Dublin was ferocious. Vickers machine guns, capable of firing 550 rounds per minute, were used against IRB-held buildings with devastating results. The Vickers .303 round, which traveled at more than twenty-five hundred feet per second, chewed up the city's gray stone buildings and tore across the scenic cobblestone streets. Dublin was not a city designed to withstand the ravages of twentieth-century warfare. At night, as the IRB tended to the wounded and dying, the British army launched pinpoint strikes against key IRB strongholds, primarily around the post office. British artillery fire lit up the dark April sky, and the sounds of machine guns rattled across the city.

The British army rushed additional troops to Dublin, unwilling to allow the IRB to use its audacious move to spark a nationwide war. The fighting lasted nearly a week until, on Saturday, April 29, the Union Jack once again flew over the entire city.

THE ORIGINAL IRA

Out of the chaos of the failed Easter Rising emerged the Irish Republican Army (IRA) as Sinn Féin's new military arm. In 1919, with IRA support, Sinn Féin established an independent parliament in Dublin and again declared Irish independence.

The British government again sent troops to crush the independence movement, but they faced stiff and unconventional resistance from the innovative legions of the IRA. Utilizing tenacious hit-and-run tactics that were difficult for the British army to defeat, the IRA was able to wage a two-year conflict. The sticking point in finding an acceptable political solution remained the six heavily Protestant counties of the north, which Britain had no plans to relinquish. IRA diehards refused to end their struggle against British rule until all the counties of the island were self-governing.

In the end, Northern Ireland came into existence in 1921 with the Government of Ireland Act. It divided the thirty-two historic counties of Ireland into two areas. Northern Ireland comprised six of the original nine Ulster counties and would remain part of the United Kingdom. The remaining twenty-six counties became the Irish Free State, which retained some ties to Britain but was largely self-governing.

Most Roman Catholics, who made up around one-third of the population of Northern Ireland, were opposed to the Government of Ireland Act. British laws restricted Catholics in

Sir Edward Carson *(left)*, a leading Protestant politician in Ulster, inspects soldiers of the Ulster Volunteer Force (UVF). Carson was urging Ulster to separate from the rest of Ireland.

these counties from holding civil service jobs and from owning businesses. Catholics didn't receive the same opportunities for housing as Protestants did. Many Catholics felt they'd become second-class citizens.

Even though most of Ireland had achieved self-rule, the IRA never gave up its desire to have one, independent Irish nation. From the late 1920s until the mid-1960s, the IRA pursued its mission with a handful of secret members. Their strategy was to carry out sporadic hit-and-run bombing attacks against British troops and the police force of Northern Ireland—the largely Protestant Royal Ulster Constabulary (RUC).

THE TROUBLES

By the late 1960s, many activists on the Irish island were calling for the use of nonviolent measures, such as peace marches, to achieve the liberation of the northern counties. Violence doomed this campaign of passive resistance. Armed Protestant militias, known as paramilitaries, often broke up Catholic peace marches. The most prominent of these groups was the Ulster Volunteer Force (UVF). The militias sometimes got support from the nearly all-Protestant RUC.

When it became clear that the RUC was not a neutral force, the British started sending army troops to keep the peace in the major cities.

In 1969 a more aggressive splinter group of the IRA, the Provisional IRA (PIRA), was formed. This clandestine terrorist group was organized into small, tightly knit cells under the leadership of an army council. The PIRA used guerrilla tactics to protect Catholics against any type of Protestant violence, military or paramilitary. The "official" IRA soon became of secondary importance to the terrorist PIRA.

Britain's response to the violence and guerrilla warfare was the internment policy, which allowed British security forces in Northern Ireland considerable freedom to arrest and detain suspected PIRA terrorists. Most of the detainees were Catholics. Consequently, the PIRA painted the British troops as an anti-Catholic occupation force. Support for the PIRA in Northern Ireland's Catholic community grew.

In August 1969, a peaceful Protestant march in Londonderry (Northern Ireland's second-largest city) became violent when Catholic activists threw stones at the marchers. Fighting ensued and soon became full-scale rioting, which, in turn, nearly escalated into all-out war.

By the late 1960s, several violent clashes had erupted between Northern Ireland's Catholic activists, who wanted union with Ireland, and its Protestant activists, who wanted to maintain ties to Britain.

THE PARAMILITARIES

The battle lines in Northern Ireland go beyond the PIRA, the British security forces, and the RUC. Several Protestant forces, loyal to Great Britain, operate as underground paramilitary terrorist groups. They have waged a terrorist war of their own to maintain British rule over Northern Ireland.

The oldest such entity is the Ulster Volunteer Force (UVF), a loyalist paramilitary group that was formed in 1966. It has waged a retaliatory terrorist war against the PIRA, often terrorizing the Roman Catholic towns and villages of Ulster through bombings, assassinations, kidnappings, extortions, and robberies. Until 1994, when the UVF agreed to a cease-fire, the group was one of the most feared organizations in Northern Ireland.

Following the signing of the 1994 UVF cease-fire, Protestant violence has primarily been carried out by the Loyalist Volunteer Force (LVF). Formed in 1996, the LVF is an extremist terrorist group that splintered from the mainstream UVF. The LVF is composed of former UVF hard-liners who have refused to accept the loyalist cease-fire.

Another major Protestant paramilitary group is the Ulster Defense Association (UDA). Formed in the early 1970s as an umbrella organization for several loyalist groups, the UDA was outlawed in 1992 because of its terrorist activities. Nevertheless, it continues to direct attacks against Catholics in Northern Ireland. ■

A member of the Ulster Defense Association (UDA)

Over the next few days, RUC members and the paramilitaries terrorized Catholic neighborhoods. The British government sent in thousands of troops to keep the peace. For many people on the island and in the United Kingdom, these events marked the advent of "the Troubles," a reference to the ongoing warfare in Northern Ireland.

The level of violence intensified following a riot in Londonderry on January 30, 1972, that became known as "Bloody Sunday." It involved Catholic anti-internment protesters, who were defying a British ban on demonstrations, and British paratroopers.

■ ■

Bloody Sunday

On Sunday, January 30, 1972, *some twenty thousand Catholic residents of Londonderry participated in a protest march against the internment policy. The British paratroopers tasked with keeping the peace in Londonderry that afternoon were the elite of the*

On what came to be known as Bloody Sunday, British troops jumped over a barbed-wire barricade in pursuit of Catholic demonstrators who had attacked them with stones and crude bombs.

British army. The march, which included women and children, was peaceful, but some young Catholic men began hurling stones and Molotov cocktails at nearby soldiers and police. And then all hell broke loose.

At 4:10 P.M., according to British military sources, the paratroopers came under fire from small arms and nail-filled bombs tossed from Bogside, a Catholic section of the city. The paratroopers, outnumbered and ill equipped to handle a hostile crowd hurling weapons at them, responded with gunfire of their own. The sounds of gunfire created panic among the protesters, who began to flee. Children and those unable to move fast were trampled. In the next thirty minutes of bedlam, the paratroopers killed thirteen people and wounded thirteen more. Most of the victims were killed with single shots to the head and torso. A suffocating cloud of tear gas hovered over Londonderry, as the screams of the wounded resonated throughout the town. "The Troubles" had reached a point of no return.

ONGOING VIOLENCE Since the 1970s, PIRA attacks have killed more than three hundred RUC police officers. The PIRA has often carried out these assassinations in front of the officers' families when the officers were off duty. The bomb has been the PIRA's weapon of choice. Bombs planted in markets, in pubs, in hotels, on street corners, and in garbage cans have resulted in the deaths of thousands of civilians and military personnel. Police and military forces in Northern Ireland have uncovered staggering numbers of weapons and explosives.

In the Republic of Ireland (which superseded the Irish Free State in 1948) and on the British mainland, the PIRA campaign has slowly but surely spread. Unlike other terrorist organizations, the goal of PIRA attacks within Britain was never for massive loss of life. In fact, after the PIRA had planted a truck bomb or another explosive device, they would often tell the authorities the location so that the targeted area could be evacuated. PIRA commanders realized indiscriminate murder would be counterproductive to their cause because it would hamper fund-raising inside the United States, a major source of money. As a result, the PIRA targeted economic and political

NORAID

According to the organization's official mission statement, Irish Northern Aid (NORAID) is a U.S. nonprofit organization founded in 1969 to provide support to the movement for Northern Ireland's independence through political action and educational outreach. It also gives financial assistance to the families of those activists who have been imprisoned or killed.

The Irish question is a sensitive topic in the United States. More than forty million Americans claim some Irish descent. Cities such as Boston, New York, and Chicago have large Irish communities where anti-British feeling flourishes and where funds are regularly collected to help what are described as Northern Irish humanitarian causes. But British law enforcement and intelligence sources have long suspected that this money is actually funneled to the PIRA to help purchase weapons and explosives. NORAID officials continue to deny these claims. ■

Graffiti on a fence in Boston, Massachusetts—a city with a large Irish American population—shows support for Sinn Féin and the Provos (PIRA).

symbols of British power and commerce, such as department stores, subway stations, and airports.

In the late 1970s and early 1980s, the PIRA stepped up its activities. On August 27, 1979, a bomb killed World War II hero Lord Louis Mountbatten and three others in Sligo, Ireland. In London, on July 22, 1982, a PIRA bomb killed eleven British soldiers during the

A British police officer stands guard outside the entrance to Harrod's, a London department store bombed by the PIRA.

ceremonial horse guards parade in Regent's Park. On December 17, 1983, a PIRA bomb exploded inside Harrod's, the fashionable London department store, killing five.

Yet the PIRA's most audacious attack failed. In October 1984, the organization tried to bomb the annual conference of the Conservative (Tory) Party. The Tories headed the British government at the time and had historically taken a hard stance against Sinn Féin. The bomb killed five and wounded dozens of others but failed to assassinate the operation's primary target—British prime minister Margaret Thatcher.

NEW THREATS TO PEACE

With decades of violence, death, and destruction as their joint legacy, the British government and Sinn Féin began intense negotiations. The talks eventually culminated in a 1997 PIRA cease-fire and the 1998 Good Friday Agreement. Islanders of all political parties got their chance to judge the accord, which won majority approval in an all-Ireland vote. Among other things, the agreement calls for most domestic affairs to be handled directly by a new Northern Ireland assembly, for reform of the RUC, and for the disarmament of all paramilitaries.

David Trimble, leader of the mainly Protestant Ulster Unionist Party, holds up a newspaper that tells the results of the 1998 vote on the Good Friday peace accords. His participation in the peace process earned him the 1998 Nobel Peace Prize, which he shared with John Hume, then leader of the mainly Catholic Social Democratic and Labor Party.

The demilitarization of the conflict and the onset of meaningful political dialogue caused extremists on both sides to surface. Perhaps the most lethal entity was the Real IRA (RIRA). A splinter group that broke away from the PIRA in 1997, the RIRA is a zealous cadre of veteran bomb makers who oppose any dialogue with the British government. The RIRA's stance is that the people of Northern Ireland should continue the use of terrorism until the British government withdraws its forces from the region once and for all.

The RIRA commenced its offensive against British forces in Northern Ireland with bombing and mortar attacks in 1998. RIRA operatives bombed shopping centers in the Northern Ireland towns of Moira, Portadown, and Banbridge. The latter attack, which injured thirty-three civilians and two RUC officers, was dwarfed by the RIRA's responsibility for the single worst atrocity of the Troubles. A powerful car bomb planted in Omagh, Northern Ireland, went off during a public celebration on August 16, 1998. It killed twenty-nine men, women, and children instantly. (Another victim died later.)

■ ■

The Omagh Bombing

A bomb is indiscriminate, *spreading death in a random fusillade of heat and shrapnel. The indiscriminate wrath of a powerful blast came to the town of Omagh, Northern Ireland, in 1998.*

The RIRA, a splinter group of the PIRA, set off the car bomb that ripped through the center of Omagh, Northern Ireland, in 1998.

Saturday, August 16, was supposed to be a peaceful summer day without any security incidents. In town for a carnival, hundreds of people walked through picturesque streets enjoying a bright, sunny day. At 2:30 P.M., in typical IRA fashion, a call came into the offices of a Belfast television station warning of a bomb set to go off in Omagh on the town's main street. Forty minutes later, as police were evacuating the area, the five-hundred-pound car bomb went off several hundred yards away. It had exploded, not on the town's main street, but at the junction of Market Street and Dublin Road, where people had gathered, thinking they were out of harm's way.

The massive explosive turned Dublin Road into a blackened fireball of death. Most of the dead were killed by the massive heat of the blast. Others were killed by shrapnel, hurled at over three thousand feet per second. The bomb did not discriminate among its victims—men or women, senior citizens or children. In all, thirty died in the blast, and more than two hundred were seriously wounded.

International outrage followed the slaughter in Omagh. The U.S. State Department declared the RIRA an international terrorist group and froze its assets in the United States. The RIRA promised to end all military operations, but in September 2000, RIRA terrorists fired an anti-tank rocket at the London headquarters of Britain's foreign intelligence service. In March 2001, they bombed the BBC's television studios in London.

In late 2002, the peace agreement hit critical snags, including a suspension of power sharing among Northern Ireland's political parties. Here, Gerry Adams, president of Sinn Féin, talks with reporters after the suspension was announced.

Despite these ongoing terrorist attacks, slow progress is being made to end the Troubles through counterterrorist policies and through negotiations. Efforts to reform the RUC, renamed the Police Service of Northern Ireland, put it at odds with hard-line members of loyalist paramilitaries, which continue to target Catholic youths. Meanwhile, the PIRA is said to be putting its extensive arsenal "beyond use."

Yet, according to British law enforcement estimates, hundreds of supporters of RIRA and its offshoots live in the Republic and in the six counties of the north. A hardened cadre of experienced PIRA terrorists is also still operative. These groups appear to be determined to continue the conflict over Northern Ireland.

Basque Nationalist Party (PNV): founded in 1895, the first party to openly work for the establishment of a Basque homeland

Batasuna: the political wing of the ETA, at one time also called Herri Batasuna. The Spanish government banned the party in 2002.

Euskadi Ta Askatasuna (ETA, Basque Fatherland and Liberty): the terrorist group formed in 1959 that has used bombings and assassinations to further the cause of Basque independence

Francisco Franco: ruler of Spain from 1939 through 1975. During his dictatorship, Franco imposed a number of anti-Basque policies.

King Juan Carlos: parliamentary monarch of Spain since 1976

Spanish government: operating from Madrid, and since 1976 the authority that has set forth policies to give Basques greater autonomy. These efforts have weakened the ETA's influence in the region.

TEDAX: the acronym for Técnicos Especialistas en Desactivación de Artefactos Explosivos, Spain's elite and effective bomb squad

THE
BASQUES
AND THE
EUSKADI TA ASKATASUNA
(ETA)

Like the conflict in Northern Ireland, the war for the creation of a Basque homeland has yet to end. The Basques are a linguistically and culturally distinct group that has lived for thousands of years in northeastern Spain and southwestern France. The mountains of the Pyrenees separate the two Basque areas, and the Bay of Biscay to the west offers access to the Atlantic Ocean. (Historically, the French Basques have been much less aggressive in pursuing a separate homeland. Most separatist activity has occurred in Spain's Basque lands.)

The Basque emblem shows both the Spanish and French provinces that make up the Basque homeland, or Euskadi in the Basque language.

HISTORICAL ROOTS

"Neither slave nor tyrant" is an old Basque motto, and the region's history of resisting the influences of foreign powers is long lived. The peoples of the area successfully stayed free of ancient Roman, Visigothic, Frankish, and Moorish political authority. Through contact with the Roman Empire, however, the Basques did accept the Roman Catholic faith, which became a bedrock

Small Basque port cities, such as Pasajes, became important shipbuilding and trading centers.

of Basque tradition. The Basques established the kingdom of Pamplona in 824, and it later developed into the kingdom of Navarre. Although from the 1500s onward, the more powerful royal houses of Spain and France brought the Basque lands under their influence, the distinctive Basque culture, language, and traditional laws, called *fueros* in Spain, were allowed to survive.

In the 1800s, the Basques took part in Spain's dynastic wars that decided which branch of the Spanish royal family should rule the country. But the side the Basques supported lost the wars. As a result, the winners abolished the fueros and suppressed other Basque traditions. The Basque lands formally became provinces of Spain.

Meanwhile, an industrial revolution was in full swing across Europe. New factories required steady supplies of iron and steel and laborers to mine the ore and make the steel. The Basque lands had good sources of iron ore, as well as a long coastline along the Bay of Biscay from where the supplies could be easily transported. The increase in jobs drew many Spanish non-Basques. The Spaniards created Spanish-speaking districts within the Basque region and formed Spanish workers' unions. These developments fostered the sense among Basques that they

Sabino Arana y Goiri founded the Basque Nationalist Party in 1895. In 1902 he was jailed for publicly supporting Spain's defeat in the Spanish-American War.

needed to preserve their unique culture.

Toward this end, in 1895, a young journalist named Sabino Arana y Goiri founded the Basque Nationalist Party (PNV, in Spanish). The party voiced the hopes of many Basques for recognition of their culture and some self-rule within Spain. But the party's goals clashed with those of hard-line Basque separatists, who wanted to create a completely independent homeland for Spain's Basques.

THE BASQUES AND FRANCO

As the Basque movements struggled to find a common voice, new political entities developed among the non-Basque Spaniards as well. By the 1930s, a group of Spaniards emerged who sought to set up a socialist government that would give more power to working-class people. These Spaniards founded the Popular Front and became known as Republicans. However, conservative Spaniards feared that the Popular Front would give too much power to the workers. These conservatives, known as Nationalists, aimed to set up a strict, law-and-order regime in Spain.

The Basques were traditionally a conservative group that tended to support conservative governments. But even though the PNV's goals seemed out of sync with the socialist aims of the Popular Front, most Basques supported the Republicans. They felt that the Republicans would reward their support by giving the Basques some self-government, though not complete independence. The Nationalists, on the other hand, had made it clear they would not share power with any of Spain's ethnic minorities.

In Spain's parliamentary elections of 1936, the PNV won a majority in the Basque provinces and put its parliamentary support behind the Popular Front, which headed a new Republican government. Within months, it had signed into law a statute granting limited autonomy to the Basque provinces. Meanwhile, however, the Nationalists—led by several Spanish army officers, including General Francisco Franco—staged a military uprising against the new government. Civil war raged throughout the country for nearly three years.

■ ■

Guernica

The church bells of Santa Maria rang *with a foreboding cadence on market day in Guernica, the cultural capital of the Basque country, that fateful Monday afternoon in 1937. Shoppers heard the first bombers as they began their descent over the Spanish city to unleash their deadly cargoes. The town square was packed with women buying fruits and vegetables, men selling their wares, and the town's gentry sitting inside cafés smoking cigars, drinking coffee, and playing cards. Guernica never stood a chance.*

General Franco had earlier asked for Germany's help in winning the Spanish civil war. So with his full approval, more than twenty-five of the German air force's most capable bombers, supported by

People walk through the rubble of Guernica after the bombing raid of the town in 1937.

dive-bombing Stukas, dumped more than 100,000 pounds of high explosives onto the town. Much of the ammunition was incendiary, setting houses, trees, and people alight. The aerial blitz was merciless. People ran for cover, but there was no place to hide. Shelters were reduced to rubble. Men, women, and children, cowering in the street, disappeared as bombs exploded on impact. Those attempting to find a spot of temporary cover from the madness were killed by fighter aircraft strafing the streets with incessant machine-gun fire.

Franco wanted the carpet bombing of Guernica to weaken the Basque people's will to continue the fight against his Nationalist forces. It marked the first use of bombers as a terrorist weapon.

■ ■

By 1939 General Franco and the Nationalists had won the civil war, and Franco had become the dictator of Spain. Basques who had taken part in the civil war were imprisoned or executed. Franco had no interest in granting any rights to an ethnic minority in Spain, especially one that had fought against him in the war. As a result, throughout his dictatorship, he severely repressed Basque culture and language, causing many Basques to flee. PNV leaders went into exile, along with many Republican leaders. This shared exile led to ongoing cooperation between the two groups—a development that angered Basques who still wanted to achieve complete independence for the Basque lands.

By 1939 General Franco had won full control of the Spanish state. One of his policies was to suppress Spain's minority cultures, including the Basques.

FOUNDING OF THE ETA | Many Basque students saw

the leaders in exile as too compromising and not willing to stand up for Basque nationalism. In 1959 a group of student activists founded the Euskadi Ta Askatasuna (ETA), meaning "Basque Fatherland and Liberty" in the Basque language. The group's stated aim was to create a completely independent homeland for Basques.

ETA activists continued to push for an independent Basque homeland despite the risk of imprisonment, torture, and execution by the Franco regime. They managed to illegally publish materials to fan the flames of Basque nationalism. Leaflets called for the removal of Spanish police from Basque areas and openly promoted the outlawed Basque language and culture. By the 1960s, with Franco's dictatorship still firmly in place, the ETA had turned to violence and terror. In 1968 ETA operatives killed Meliton Manzanas, who headed the secret police in the Basque city of San Sebastian. In December 1973, they assassinated Admiral Luis Carrero Blanco, Spain's premier and the man seen by many as Franco's most likely successor.

A Political Assassination

Luis Carrero Blanco was a unique man in Spain. *He was trusted by Franco, a dictator whose nature was not to trust anyone at all. Basque terrorists had been looking for a suitable political target to assassinate for quite some time. But Franco, always wary of assassination plots, was too well protected. Carrero Blanco was a good second choice.*

The terrorists tasked with killing Franco's closest confidant didn't want to leave clues behind. The dictator's wrath against the minority Basque population would be severe if the crime were linked to the ETA.

Because of their work as dynamiters in local mines, the Basques were known throughout Europe as legendary explosives experts. In December 1973, that expertise was used with great effectiveness. Operatives placed a powerful car bomb underneath Blanco's usual parking spot near his office in Madrid, Spain's capital. The terrorists had bored through the spot's concrete covering, had dug a pit for the bomb, and then had repaved the spot. The bomb was so

The force of the bomb that killed Premier Carrero Blanco created a huge hole in the street.

powerful that, when it exploded, it lifted Carrero Blanco's sedan ten feet off the ground and obliterated everything—including Carrero Blanco—inside the vehicle. The murder of Admiral Luis Carrero Blanco was a bold and audible statement to the people of Spain that this new Basque movement was willing and able to carry out attacks against people at the highest levels of power.

In 1976, following Franco's death and the long-awaited restoration of democracy to Spain, many of the PNV exiles returned. The new constitutional monarchy under King Juan Carlos granted considerable political autonomy to the country's ethnic regions. The Spanish government allowed the Basque areas to have their own parliament and granted them a hand in deciding issues such as taxation and education. The Basque language was again taught to youngsters.

But the members of the ETA, a radical minority in the region, believed that autonomy was a far cry from an independent Basque homeland. They vowed to win an independent state by continuing their reign of violence and terror. Meanwhile, the ETA founded its own political party, Batasuna.

ETA ACTIVITIES

The ETA has used bombings, assassinations, and kidnappings, mainly of politicians and police officers, in its terrorist campaign. In 1995 the ETA even attempted to kill King Juan Carlos and José Maria Aznar, then leader of the conservative Popular Party. (Aznar would later become Spain's prime minister.)

The words *errefuxiatuak* (refugee) and *Euskadin Libre* (free Euskadi) appear on part of a Basque nationalist mural. The soldiers each wear the flags of France *(left)* and Spain *(right)*, suggesting the antiseparatist cooperation between the two governments.

An Attempt on King Juan Carlos

The apartment smelled like stale coffee *and stank from ashtrays that hadn't been emptied in days. The two men inside were told not to make noise, not to go outside, and not to do anything that would attract the attention of the neighbors and the authorities. The refrigerator had been stocked with food, and the two men had enough cigarettes to last them a month. If they got bored, they could watch soccer on TV or listen to music on the transistor radio in the bedroom. The apartment was dark, even though the August sun was shining brightly in Majorca, off Spain's Mediterranean coast. It would be easier to hit their target in the sunlight, the two men thought, and harder for the bodyguards to see the rifle if the apartment were kept dark.*

The job was simple—to assassinate King Juan Carlos with a shot to the head from a Finnish-made Sako .308 rifle as he boarded the royal yacht moored five hundred yards away from the apartment. The two men were the best operatives the ETA could spare—calm, cool, and dead-on shots. One man would act as the observer, scouting out the target and ranging it. The other would pull the trigger, rechambering his rifle only if the first round did not kill the king.

But the ETA cell responsible for the operation had been compromised in late July. French intelligence had learned of the plot, and they had informed their Spanish allies. On August 11, 1995, less than an hour before the king was supposed to go sailing with his family, a thirty-man Spanish force stormed the apartment. Clad in black coveralls, their faces covered by masks, and MP5 submachine guns in their hands, the men breached the fortified door with explosives and apprehended the assassins. The king sailed that afternoon, unaware of

King Juan Carlos and Queen Sofia

how close he had come to being in the crosshairs of a Finnish rifle.

In 1997 and 1998, the ETA targeted many politicians, including elected officials from the Popular Party. In July 1997, ETA members kidnapped and killed councillor Miguel Angel Blanco. About a year later, an ETA car bomb took the life of councillor Manuel Zamarreño. The government's reaction was to jail members of the Herri Batasuna. Overall, ETA attacks in Spain have killed about one thousand people. Almost half these casualties have been police and security personnel.

The violence has caused fear and foreboding in many of Spain's major cities, but the ETA's bombing campaign has failed to make life

While destructive, ETA car bombs have not succeeded in disrupting life in Spain's major cities.

unlivable in the country. The ongoing efforts of Spain's internal police and special operations counterterrorist team have thwarted many bomb attacks.

Another Day on the Job

Traffic has come to a grinding halt on the congested *Avenida Ciudad de Barcelona in downtown Madrid, and motorists know why. There is another bomb scare.*

Inside a secure perimeter within the street, a handful of men peer through field glasses at a car parked near the railway station. The car was reported stolen a few days earlier in the Basque city of Bilbao. An alert traffic cop saw several wires protruding from the car's glove compartment, and this was reason enough to call in the experts.

Following standard operating procedures, one officer guides a small robot, armed with a shotgun, to the car via remote control. His first move is to check the trunk, where most explosives tend to be planted. *A television monitor within the perimeter gives him a hazy picture of what's going on. Raising the gun's barrel remotely, the officer fires a round through the trunk's lock. Peering at the sketchy black-and-white TV screen, he sees suspicious items inside the trunk—a briefcase, a tire with some tools inside, and a canvas bag. The robot won't be able to give the officer any more information, so with little choice, he realizes his partner will have to go in manually.*

The senior bomb technician puts on the cumbersome protective suit. It weighs eighty pounds and constricts movement yet shields him against explosions. A respirator, protected by a domelike helmet complete with a Plexiglas visor, allows the officer to breathe. Completing the technician's gear is a round metal shield.

The bomb technician is trained to focus solely on the problem at hand and on his checklist of standard operating procedures. Thoughts of family and personal safety only cloud the work that needs to be done. The walk toward the suspicious car is a solitary exercise in courage and experience. Standing by the canvas bag, the officer deems the sack to hold nothing more than personal belongings. Overcome by the exhaustion of wearing the massive suit, he drops to one knee and throws his partner the thumbs-up sign that all is clear.

It is just another routine day for the officers of TEDAX, Spain's national bomb squad. In the international bomb

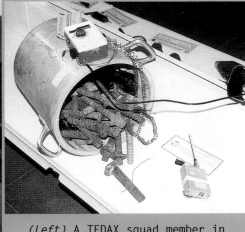

(*Left*) A TEDAX squad member in full gear. (*Above*) One of the many devices TEDAX has dismantled.

disposal community, the TEDAX unit is considered the elite. Since its inception in 1975, TEDAX has handled thousands of pounds of explosive devices and has rendered safe some thirty-five hundred actual devices. There are TEDAX teams in twenty-six cities throughout the country, but the men in Madrid are its elite and the busiest.

■ ■

In addition to the TEDAX units, the Spanish government has sent national and local police forces to the Basque region to discover and confiscate hidden supplies of arms. These forces have monitored border crossings where ETA commanders have shuttled to and from safe havens in France. More than 430 ETA operatives have been arrested and are currently in Spanish prisons.

Despite the violence it has perpetrated, the ETA has also succeeded in publicizing the plight and cultural significance of the Basque people and of achieving some political concessions. There is

A BOMB BUILDER

Basque terrorist bombs are highly complex and built to kill any police officer brave enough to attempt to neutralize them. Most terrorist bombs in Spain pack enough of a blast to pepper an armored car full of holes. The ETA's car bombs are booby-trapped with intricate trip wires—including photoelectric switches that explode when exposed to daylight and radio-controlled switches that go off after the bomb technician thinks the triggering mechanism has been dismantled. The ETA has even placed bombs inside expensive radio-controlled motor cars to target the bomb-disposal technicians.

One of ETA's best bomb builders was Francisco Javier Garcia Gaztelu, who started out assassinating elected officials and police officers throughout the Basque region and then quickly rose through the ranks of the ETA. Considered a coldhearted fanatic by even hard-line ETA operatives, Gaztelu played a personal role in the kidnapping and murder of a prominent Spanish politician in 1997. Moving between France and Spain, Gaztelu assumed command of the ETA in September 2000 after French and Spanish counterterrorists arrested twenty of the ETA's top field commanders. (He has since been arrested by French police.) ■

Carrying anti-ETA signs, thousands of Spaniards marched in protest of
renewed ETA violence in the early 2000s.

greater autonomy in Spain's Basque region than at any other time in
recent history, and the Basques, for the most part, govern and police
themselves. Many schools in the Basque region teach almost exclusively
in Basque.

But the violence has often silenced the message of Basque
independence. In January 2000, following a series of ETA car bombs in
the capital, more than 200,000 people marched in downtown Madrid to
call for the ETA to end its bombing campaign once and for all. Support
for Batasuna also waned, followed by the central government's banning
of the party in 2002. Meanwhile, the Spanish government's efforts to
recognize some Basque rights seem to have weakened the ETA's
position, but this terrorist organization has yet to publicly abandon
its goal.

Abdullah Ocalan: leader of the Partia Karkaren Kurdistan (PKK) since 1978, in jail in Turkey since 1999

Kurdistan: the region inhabited by Kurds that overlaps the borders of Syria, Iraq, Iran, and Turkey

Marxist: a person who supports the economic and political theories of Karl Marx. He believed the historic struggle between the workers and the bosses would eventually result in a working-class rebellion that would usher in a workers' paradise.

Mustafa Kemal (later known as Atatürk, 1881–1938): the founder of the Republic of Turkey

Partia Karkaren Kurdistan (PKK, Kurdistan Workers Party): the political wing and guerrilla organization that has been waging war against the Turkish government since 1984. In 2002 the PKK changed its name to the Congress for Freedom and Democracy in Kurdistan (KADEK).

Treaty of Lausanne: the 1923 treaty that established the Republic of Turkey and divided up Kurdistan

Treaty of Sèvres: the 1920 treaty that was supposed to result in the establishment of an independent Kurdish state. The treaty was never implemented.

Turkish government: operating from Ankara, the authority that has been waging war against the PKK

THE
KURDISTAN WORKERS PARTY
(PKK)

The vast area known as Kurdistan covers about 230,000 square miles of harsh, mountainous terrain in parts of Turkey, Iraq, Iran, and Syria. The Kurds are the fourth largest ethnic group in the Middle East, after the Arabs, the Persians, and the Turks.

This unforgiving landscape has spawned another national liberation group, the Kurdistan Workers Party (PKK). Based in southern Turkey, the PKK has waged a seemingly endless—and bloody—war in search of an autonomous homeland for the Kurdish people.

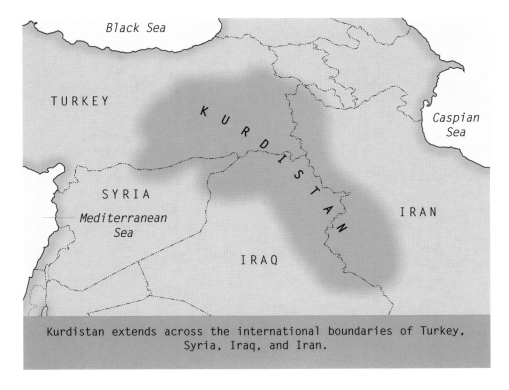

Kurdistan extends across the international boundaries of Turkey, Syria, Iraq, and Iran.

HISTORICAL ROOTS

The Kurds are a unique fusion of Middle Eastern peoples and cultures. The earliest evidence of a unified and distinct Kurdish culture is more than eight thousand years old, with small Kurdish kingdoms in existence by 300 B.C.

By the late A.D. 600s, Arab armies were sweeping through the Middle East, bringing the Islamic faith with them. The Kurds eventually adopted the religion and were able to continue to develop their own culture within the larger Islamic empire. They established tribes that operated independently at the local level.

In the 1100s and 1200s, Turkish nomads who also followed the Islamic faith arrived in the area. By the late 1400s, they had created the Ottoman Empire, which politically dominated vast segments of the Middle East and parts of Africa. One area that the Ottomans did not control was the Persian Empire (modern Iran), which lay just east of the Ottoman Empire. This swath of land at the farthest eastern extent of the Ottoman Empire and the farthest western extent of the Persian Empire was home to the Kurds, who called the region Kurdistan.

In a major battle in 1514, the Ottomans defeated the Persians, who were trying to expand their empire. Kurdish lands became a buffer

A late-sixteenth-century artwork from a Kurdish manuscript depicts the Battle of Chaldiran in 1514.

region between the two empires. The Ottoman sultan (ruler) divided his section of the Kurdish lands into provinces but allowed local leaders to govern them as hereditary rulers. In exchange, the local leaders agreed to monitor unrest in the region, to fight alongside the sultan if needed, and to pay taxes. (In Persia the shah (ruler) took the opportunity to violently subdue the Kurds.)

In Ottoman lands, the arrangement persisted until the early 1800s, when several parts of the empire—Egypt and Greece, for example—succeeded in gaining some measure of self-rule. To forestall further weakening of Ottoman authority, the sultan began appointing Turkish governors to rule Kurdistan. By 1867 the Ottomans had systematically eradicated local Kurdish rule.

Kurdish cavalry troops helped the Ottoman Empire fight wars in the late 1800s and early 1900s.

THE KURDS AND THE OTTOMAN EMPIRE

Meanwhile, outside powers—the Russians, the British, and the French among them—were eyeing Ottoman lands. To protect the empire, especially in the vulnerable buffer zone, the Ottomans wanted to quash the nationalist hopes of its many ethnic minorities, including the Kurds. Much to the annoyance of the sultan, these nationalist hopes were in step with the movement of the Young Turks, who wanted to found a Turkish state in which all people, including the Kurds, would have equal rights. In 1908 the Young Turks overthrew the sultan and set up a constitutional government that worked through the sultan's brother. The new government quickly reneged on its early promises and began outlawing non-Turkish publications, schools, and political organizations.

Not long afterward, World War I (1914–1918) broke out and pitted Ottoman Turkey against the very powers that had been eyeing its territory. Meanwhile, the Kurds and other minority ethnic groups continued to press for independence. Appealing to their common Islamic faith, the Turks convinced the Kurds to fight the non-Islamic allied powers. The Kurds believed they'd receive benefits in so doing, but in 1917 the Turks took harsh steps to try to end Kurdish nationalism.

■ ■

1917: A Turkish Raid

The villagers knew when the Turkish army was coming. Just after dawn, an eerie calm would set in, followed by the unmistakable roar of horses, hundreds of horses, galloping in formation down dirt roads, moving in for what all knew would be a bloodbath. If the troops had made their camp close to the village and word was spread by messenger, the village's men would have a

Turkish soldiers during World War I

chance to flee into the hills. The women, the children, and those too old to flee were left to the Turkish soldiers, who were paid and trained to have no mercy. The Kurds were renowned for their mountain warfare skills, but when they were outnumbered and poorly armed, they were merely a ragtag opponent for the Turks' Mauser rifles, heavy cannons, and cavalry fire.

The Turks singled out villages that were known as hotbeds of Kurdish nationalism for destruction. Kurdish men were beheaded along mountain roadways. Women were raped. Children were orphaned. Those left alive were often imprisoned or forced to flee, ushering in a long refugee crisis.

■ ■

While the Ottoman forces were trying to stamp out Kurdish nationalism, their fortunes in the world war were not going well. Britain was beating Ottoman forces on the Arabian Peninsula and in parts of southwestern Asia, and France was taking over other parts of southwestern Asia and countries along the Aegean Sea. Rather than sign a surrender, the Young Turks went into hiding and left that role for the former sultan's brother. He signed a peace agreement with the allied powers, many of which were coveting the newly discovered deposits of oil within Ottoman territory.

The Young Turks, under their leader Mustafa Kemal, reappeared after the war to protest the allied takeover of Turkish land. The Kurds, who had mostly fought alongside the Turks in the war, lacked a charismatic leader to speak for the idea of Kurdistan. Although there was a strong desire for a Kurdish state, no central or organized group existed to push for it. The allied powers thought an independent Kurdistan would be a buffer between Turkey and the oil-rich lands of the former Ottoman Empire. The Turks needed Kurdish military support to hang on to Turkey. As a result, the Kurds became pawns between the Turks and the Allies, with each side promising the Kurds more rights and land in exchange for their support.

To settle this dispute, the Treaty of Sèvres was drawn up between the allied powers and Turkey in 1921. Although it divided up the historic Kurdish lands between Britain and France, a small portion of the region was to become an independent Kurdish state.

A KURDISH STATE

At the end of World War I, the victors—including Britain and France—set about carving up the former Ottoman Empire, as well as setting up the League of Nations. This new organization was meant to provide a forum for resolving international disputes.

The victors' efforts ignited the dream of a Kurdish state, which was further inflamed by certain provisions in the Treaty of Sèvres. It seemed to set forth conditions under which such a state might be possible.

SECTION III. Kurdistan. Article 62. A Commission . . . shall draft within six months from the coming into force of the present Treaty a scheme of local autonomy for the predominantly Kurdish areas lying east of the Euphrates [River], south of the southern boundary of Armenia, . . . and north of the frontier of Turkey with Syria and Mesopotamia [modern Iraq]. . . . If unanimity cannot be secured on any question, it will be referred by the members of the Commission to their respective governments. . . .

SECTION III. Kurdistan. Article 63. The Turkish Government hereby agrees to accept and execute the decisions of both the Commissions mentioned in Article 62 within three months from their communication to the said Government.

SECTION III. Kurdistan. Article 64. If within one year from the coming into force of the present Treaty the Kurdish peoples within the areas defined in Article 62 shall address themselves to the Council of the League of Nations in such a manner as to show that a majority of the population of these areas desires independence from Turkey, and if the Council then considers that these peoples are capable of such independence and recommends that it should be granted to them, Turkey hereby agrees to execute such a recommendation, and to renounce all rights and title over these areas. ∎

The victorious European powers met after World War I. They stated their support for a Kurdish state but were even more interested in how to divide up the Ottoman Empire.

The treaty's provisions were never enforced, however. The Young Turks overthrew the sultan once and for all and refused to sign the treaty. The Treaty of Lausanne, signed on June 24, 1923, divided up Kurdish lands among Turkey, Syria, Iraq, and Persia and formally established the Turkish republic. The Kurdish tribes throughout former Ottoman Empire were offered no hope of political independence.

1920s to 1960s

Turkey, bordered by Syria to the south and Iraq to the east, viewed Kurdish nationalistic aspirations as a threat to its own national security. Some twelve million Kurdish men, women, and children were living in Turkey, which had emerged from World War I in unstable economic and political condition. To consolidate power, Kemal (renamed Atatürk, meaning Father of the Turks) wanted to make a Turkish-only state. To achieve this goal, he believed it was necessary for all other groups to assimilate. In fact, the Turkish government considered the Kurds merely Mountain Turks and not a separate minority.

Throughout the 1920s and 1930s, the new Turkish government banned the Kurdish language and Kurdish schools. It was even illegal to admit that a Kurdish culture existed. Kurdish rebels fought back, starting uprisings in various parts of Turkish Kurdistan. The Turks responded by

Atatürk, Turkey's first president, envisioned a state in which all ethnic minorities, including Kurds, would be absorbed into Turkish culture.

sending in troops. The revolts continued, however, and the Turkish government responded with even more force.

By the late 1940s and early 1950s, Turkey was hoping to receive financial and military support from the United States. To court U.S. favor, Turkey relaxed some of its repressive measures. Kurdish politicians were allowed to hold public office (but only if they didn't acknowledge their ethnicity), and Kurdish could be spoken in private. The Turks received U.S. aid and allowed U.S. military bases to be built on Turkish soil.

Meanwhile, Kurds in other countries stepped up their efforts to gain rights and recognition. Worried that these activities would spill over into Turkey, the Turkish government cracked down on expressions of Kurdish political will and culture. These attempts only served to incite Kurds in Turkey to further opposition. Kurdish political groups held meetings and demonstrations, and Kurdish activists raised issues about economic development and personal freedoms.

THE FOUNDING OF THE PKK

Turkey experienced considerable political turmoil in the 1960s and 1970s. Politicians within the right wing wanted to hold true to the Turkish-only goals of Atatürk, who had died in 1938. Politicians within the left wing had adopted a more liberal political view that, among other things, wanted to give more freedoms to Turkey's minorities.

The Partia Karkaren Kurdistan (PKK, or Kurdistan Workers Party) was born out of Turkey's left-wing student organizations. Founded in 1978 by Abdullah Ocalan, the PKK primarily aimed to foment a violent Marxist revolution in Turkey that would usher in a Communist state. Members of the PKK saw themselves as carrying the torch of national liberation with a brash Marxist approach.

IRAQ'S KURDS

The Kurds of Iraq, like those who live in Turkey, have long dreamed of an independent Kurdistan. By the 1960s, Mustafa Barzani, founder of the Kurdistan Democratic Party (KDP), had established a Kurdish territory in northern Iraq.

Meanwhile, the Baath Party, which preached an all-Arab ideology, had come to power in Iraq. The party viewed the minority Kurds as a threat and blamed Iraq's political instability on Kurdish nationalistic aspirations. By the 1970s, the Iraqi army had launched a military campaign against Kurdish towns and villages.

Led by the KDP, Iraqi Kurds responded with guerrilla attacks on Iraqi government forces and installations. The Iraqi military, one of the strongest in the region, had little trouble defeating the KDP. The battered Kurdish leadership sought refuge in nearby Iran. Intermittent fighting continued for the next twenty years.

In 1984 then-Iraqi leader Saddam Hussein stepped up the fighting, turning his armed forces against the Kurds once again. The Iraqi campaign was furious and was typified by the March 16, 1988, poisoned gas attack on the town of Halabja. The three-day attack left 5,000 dead and 30,000 injured. Halabja was the largest, but not the only, Kurdish town to be attacked with chemical weapons. The more than two decades of campaigns against the Iraqi Kurds have resulted in the destruction of more than four thousand villages and the deaths of as many as 250,000 Kurds. ■

Iraqi chemical weapons attacks on thousands of Iraqi Kurdish villages are believed to have killed 250,000 people in the 1980s.

Ocalan viewed the changing world of the late 1970s as the Kurds' greatest opportunity for self-determination, and he was determined to use all force necessary, including terrorist activities, to achieve his goal. Meanwhile, Kurdish groups with similar hopes were also cropping up in northern Iraq and in northwestern Iran.

After clashes erupted between left-wing Kurds and right-wing security forces in Turkey's Kurdish areas, the Turkish government imposed martial law in the region. Turkish troops were again patrolling Kurdistan, and the government was arresting Kurd terrorists suspected of nationalist activity.

In the early 1980s, Ocalan escaped to Syria, a longtime regional rival of Turkey. The Syrian government (which calls the landmass that includes both Lebanon and Syria Greater Syria) allowed Ocalan and his PKK operatives to openly train with Syrian-supported terrorist groups. The PKK resorted to robberies, extortion, and even the lucrative opium trade to finance its activities.

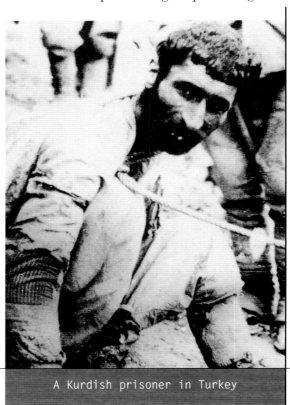

A Kurdish prisoner in Turkey

PKK Training in Greater Syria

No signs dotted the east-west highway that connected Beirut, Lebanon, and Damascus, Syria. The nearby terrorist training camp didn't appear on any map either. Yet inside the poppy-rich fields of Lebanon's Bekáa Valley, far from outside view and camouflaged by rows of trees, lay one of the Middle East's busiest training camps. The young men and women who ventured from the mountains of Kurdistan or from the slums of Kurdish cities

Abdullah Ocalan shakes hands with PKK terrorist recruits being trained in the Bekáa Valley.

into the valley didn't think of themselves as terrorists. They called themselves freedom fighters, even though the curriculum at the camp included improvised explosive devices, cold-killing, sniping, and urban combat obstacle courses.

The Mahsun Korkmaz Academy in the Bekáa Valley was the area's largest PKK training camp. Barbed wire and watchtowers surrounded a series of buildings and tents, where the students slept and prepared for the arduous three months of commando-like instruction. Names were never used in the camp. Fraternization between the male and female students was strictly forbidden.

The day commenced at dawn and usually lasted well past midnight. The instructors—Libyan explosives experts, Syrian martial arts instructors, and Palestinian combat course masters—were the best money could buy. The teachers instructed the young PKK operatives to show no mercy. They were taught to be killing machines that even the cruelty of the Turkish secret service or the Turkish special forces couldn't break. They were trained to liberate Kurdistan no matter what the cost.

PKK supporters wave flags and placards at a rally in Lebanon.

ONGOING VIOLENCE

The desire to create an independent Kurdish state was a powerful dream that Ocalan used as a recruiting tool. By 1987 he had managed to bring thousands of operatives into the ranks of the PKK and to sign on thousands more as sympathizers. In a matter of years and with minimal financial support, Ocalan had created the seeds of a popular uprising.

But while most Kurds wanted self-rule, they didn't necessarily want it within a Communist state. The PKK began a brutal terrorist war to destabilize the Turkish government and cause revolution. This war also targeted Kurdish groups unwilling to join the PKK's war against Turkey or to abide by the PKK's Marxist ideology.

ABDULLAH OCALAN

Born in eastern Turkey in 1948, Abdullah Ocalan developed his Marxist leanings while enrolled as a student in Ankara University in Turkey. By 1973 he had formed his first small group of Kurdish militants, whose goal was to start a socialist revolution in Turkey. By 1978 he had formally established the PKK.

For many years, Ocalan's PKK won considerable support from Syria, where young Kurdish operatives trained to become effective terrorists. Meanwhile, Ocalan blended his socialist stance with the dream of Kurdish independence—a move that earned him broader support among the Kurdish people.

In 1998, after the threat of a Turkish-Syrian clash forced Syria to close its PKK camps, Ocalan fled to Russia, which eventually expelled him. This move forced him to flee to Italy and then to Greece, whose government helped Ocalan escape to Kenya. Turkish officials apprehended Ocalan in Africa in February 1999. A Turkish tribunal convicted him of treason and sentenced him to death, a decision commuted to life imprisonment in 2002. Isolated on the Turkish island of Imrali, Ocalan continues to garner support and sympathy from Kurds. In December 2002, Kurdish activists launched an international initiative to win his release. ■

Soon after his capture in 1999, Ocalan was under the close watch of a masked guard on his flight back to Turkey.

A PKK Raid

The attack came at night, when the village's guard was least alert. The attackers were armed only with run-of-the-mill assault rifles, machine guns, grenades, and daggers. But they were enough to perpetrate a massacre, enough to instill fear in the local residents. Kurdish villagers in Iraq's northwestern regions were used to terror, but the attack by fellow Kurds displayed a new type of brutality yet unseen in the conflict.

At 11:00 P.M., on the night of October 27, 1997, PKK operatives raided four rural mountain villages in Iraqi Kurdistan with untold ferocity and barbarity. Many victims were shot point blank in the head. Others were burned alive when their homes were set alight. In all, fourteen people died, including ten small children.

A village guard prepares for a PKK terrorist attack.

For the PKK, the raids were payback. A local Iraqi Kurdish clan had recently defeated PKK terrorists in a fight, and the humiliation on the battlefield could not go unpunished. In perpetrating its attacks, the PKK fulfilled its main objective of terrorizing the local population to force cooperation or to suffer the consequences.

In the late 1990s, the PKK attacked Turkish sites at home and abroad. Turkish diplomats, financial institutions, and airline offices in Europe all became targets. The PKK also singled out Turkey's tourism

Immediately after Ocalan's capture, the PKK vowed to raise the level of violence. Suicide bombers attacked Turkey's cities, aiming their activities mostly at military targets but injuring hundreds of civilians as well. Here, experts examine the remains of a military bus blown up by a female PKK suicide bomber. Her action killed three and wounded more than twenty people.

industry, one of the country's primary sources of foreign income, by bombing tourist sites and kidnapping tourists in the major city of Istanbul and at Turkish seaside resorts.

In February 1999, Turkish counterterrorist commandos captured Abdullah Ocalan in Kenya following a cross-continent chase from Europe. Ocalan was brought back to Turkey to face a military tribunal. He was tried, convicted, and sentenced to death. This decision was converted to a life-imprisonment sentence, and Ocalan is serving out his sentence in a Turkish island prison.

Ocalan's capture seriously hampered the PKK's operational ability. Within months, the PKK had announced its intention to abandon the fight for Kurdish self-rule. In 2002 the group changed its name to the Congress for Freedom and Democracy in Kurdistan (KADEK). Ocalan continued as the group's leader. Meanwhile, the organization still maintains an extensive terrorist network inside Kurdistan and in Europe.

Indian government: operating from New Delhi, the most populous democratic power in the region with a large Tamil population of its own. India was involved in the Sri Lankan conflict between 1987 and 1990.

Janatha Vimukthi Peramuna (JVP, People's Liberation Front): a terrorist Sinhalese group that started its antigovernment and anti-Tamil campaign in the early 1970s. Sri Lankan security forces had killed the main JVP leaders by 1989.

Liberation Tigers of Tamil Eelam (LTTE): the largest and most militant Tamil secessionist group in Sri Lanka

Sri Lankan government: operating from Colombo, the authority that has fought the LTTE and other terrorist groups on the island

SWRD Bandaranaike: the founder of the Sri Lanka Freedom Party, which advocated a "Sinhala-only" platform

Vellupillai Prabhakaran: the founder and leader of the LTTE

THE TIGERS OF SRI LANKA

The island of Sri Lanka is located off the southeastern coast of India in the Indian Ocean. Called Ceylon until 1972, the island has long been inhabited by two main ethnic groups—the Buddhist Sinhalese and the Hindu Tamil. The Portuguese occupied Ceylon in the sixteenth century, and the Dutch took it over in the seventeenth century. Britain eventually gained control of the island from the Dutch, and Ceylon became a colony of the British Empire in 1802. Lying close to Africa and India, Ceylon became one of the empire's strategic outposts, as well as the site for some of its most lucrative tea plantations.

The island nation of eighteen million inhabitants has been beset by racial and religious strife between the Sinhalese majority and the Tamil minority. The Sinhalese are the largest ethnic and religious group on the island, comprising approximately 70 percent of the population. They trace back their presence on the island some twenty-five hundred years and

The British Lipton company grew tea on plantations in Ceylon in the 1800s.

dominate the southern half of the island, as well as the capital city of Colombo. The ancestors of the Tamil, who make up only 10 percent of Sri Lanka's population, arrived from India about one thousand years ago. Their descendants reside primarily in northern and eastern Sri Lanka. (Another category of Tamil—Estate Tamil—make up 10 percent of Sri Lanka's population. They are descendants of Indian plantation laborers whom the British sent to the island in the 1800s.)

EARLY CONFLICTS

In the years following World War II (1939–1945), Britain found itself unable to sustain its far-flung empire. Many of its colonies, including Ceylon, pursued independence. The drive for self-rule united all the ethnic groups on the island. After the British granted Ceylon independence in 1948, however, these unifying sentiments disintegrated along racial lines.

Government programs that relocated Sinhalese to less-crowded areas inhabited by Tamil exacerbated racial divisions. Sinhalese saw the Tamil minority, many of whom the British had welcomed into the colony's bureaucracy, as having too much power. The Ceylonese government required the Estate Tamil to document their arrival on the island or lose their citizenship. Most Estate Tamil were unable to provide the required information and lost many of their civil rights.

In 1956 the Sinhalese Sri Lanka Freedom Party (SLFP) won a majority. The SLFP's top political platform called for the establishment of Sinhala (the language of the Sinhalese) as the country's sole official language to be used in government and in the courts. This move would make it nearly impossible for most Tamil (whose language is also called

British officials, Sri Lankan leaders, and other heads of state mark the occasion of Ceylon's independence in 1948.

SWRD Bandaranaike discusses his Sinhala-only views at a rally in 1955. His party's victory in Ceylon's 1956 elections ushered in a number of pro-Sinhalese policies.

Tamil) to exercise any political power. The victory of the SLFP and its leader, SWRD Bandaranaike, worried the minority populations. Some Sinhalese also attempted to make Buddhism the country's official religion and to impose restrictive quotas for minorities in the fields of higher education and the civil service.

Militant Tamil, supported by a large population of Tamil in nearby southern India, set the stage for violent confrontations in the 1950s and 1960s. Racial rioting— often protesting the Sinhala-Only Act—ensued, as did political turmoil.

■ ■

Bandaranaike's Assassination

The government of Prime Minister SWRD Bandaranaike had attempted—unsuccessfully—to stem the political and religious turmoil inside Ceylon. But extremists within his own camp, who felt that the government wasn't doing enough to eradicate Tamil culture from the country's day-to-day life, demanded blood—the blood of the prime minister.

On the morning of September 25, 1959, Talduwe Somarama Thero, a Buddhist monk, had an appointment to meet Prime Minister Bandaranaike at his ministerial residence. Bandaranaike was in the act of paying his respects to the religious caller when suddenly Thero produced a .38 caliber revolver that had been

Children pay their respects to the tomb of Prime Minister Bandaranaike, who was assassinated by a Buddhist monk in 1959.

hidden in his robes. Taking aim, the monk fired a six-round clip at the prime minister, hitting him in the stomach. The next day, although he had survived emergency surgery, Bandaranaike was dead—the first of many political leaders in Sri Lanka to fall victim to an assassin's bullet.

The next major outbreak of violence was in 1971, when the Sinhalese group Janatha Vimukthi Peramuna (JVP, or People's Liberation Front) attempted to seize control of the island. The most heartless JVP terrorists were highly educated, jobless Sinhalese young men and women who thought the Sinhalese-controlled government wasn't doing enough to improve their economic circumstances. The government cracked down on the JVP, killing thousands, while JVP violence took its toll on Sinhalese civil servants and Tamil workers.

JVP Violence

Frustrated by a stagnant economy, *JVP terrorists launched an armed rebellion against the government and people of Sri Lanka* *in the 1970s with a ferocity never before seen on the tropical island. Much of the violence was carried out by mobs. Groups of young, rural thugs—wielding machetes, daggers, and assault rifles— attacked police stations, banks, or any symbols of governmental authority. Civil servants, eking out a meager living in government jobs, were often ambushed as they conducted their day-to-day jobs.*

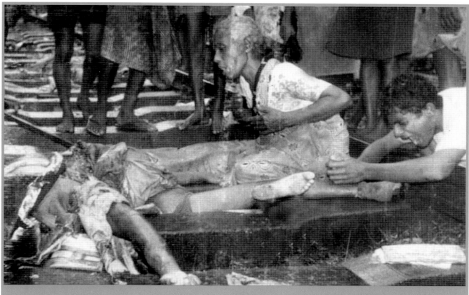

JVP terrorists targeted Tamil civilians and Sri Lankan government workers.

Some were beheaded. Others were shot to death and their bodies set afire. The terrorists' strategy was to make average citizens fear for their lives.

At the same time, several Tamil separatist groups of differing ideologies began to emerge in Tamil areas of the island. Tamil émigrés living in North America (primarily Canada) and in western Europe financed and supported many of these groups. These Tamil liberation movements sought the establishment of an independent Tamil homeland in the north and the east—areas of the island where they were the overwhelming majority. The most prominent of these groups was the Liberation Tigers of Tamil Eelam (LTTE, also known as the Tamil Tigers).

FOUNDING OF THE LTTE | The

LTTE was founded by Vellupillai Prabhakaran, a Tamil guerrilla warlord who shot to fame in May 1975 when he personally pulled the trigger on the gun that killed Alfred Duriappah, the Tamil mayor of Jaffna (the major city in the north). As part of the local government, Duriappah was working with the Sri Lankan national government. Tamil separatists saw him as a traitor to the Tamil cause.

Vellupillai Prabhakaran

Duriappah's Assassination

As targets go, *Alfred Duriappah—the Tamil mayor of Jaffna and a political symbol—was a marked man. An earlier attempt on the mayor had missed him by moments. The second attempt on Duriappah's life was fatal.*

As the mayor was driven to a city temple to worship, four young men, lying in wait, rushed his official car with pistols drawn. Duriappah's protectors were caught off guard. The fusillade of handgun fire was point-blank and unrelenting. Mortally wounded, Duriappah fell out of his car and to the ground in a pool of blood.

The state's security services spread a dragnet throughout the

Jaffa's mayor Alfred Duriappah *(right)* became a target for LTTE violence. His assassination was the first of many political murders by LTTE operatives.

country to find the four fleeing assassins. Rewards were offered, suspects were tortured, and eventually three of the gunmen were apprehended and imprisoned. The fourth, Vellupillai Prabhakaran, got away.

Building the LTTE along military lines, Prabhakaran used tried-and-true guerrilla teams in the field, but he also put secret forces into action. Their dedication to the cause was unflinching. His fierce fanaticism was also turned on his own ethnic group, when he and his forces began terrorizing Tamil who were reluctant to support his cause. Financial support for the group's activities mainly came from heroin trafficking.

The LTTE attracts young, educated Tamil men and women who have lost faith in the Sri Lankan political system.

TAMIL CONNECTION

L TTE heroin trafficking began in the early 1980s, after the Soviet invasion of Afghanistan compromised long-established heroin routes. Industrious and with émigrés around the world, the Tamil were ideal newcomers to the trade. But eventually the LTTE realized that it could not reap huge profits by selling domestically to a cash-strapped population. They focused on Europe and North America.

Officials arrested Tamil drug traffickers in Italy, France, Germany, Spain, and Switzerland. One of the most lucrative Tamil heroin routes was through Canada, where a sizable Tamil population thrived in the country's largest cities. Heroin from Pakistan, Afghanistan, Iran, and India was funneled through Tamil brokers and smuggled into Canada and then into the United States. Although U.S., Canadian, and European law enforcement officials have arrested hundreds of Tamil drug smugglers, profits from heroin continue to be the LTTE's primary source of cash. ■

Starting in 1978, the group commenced its armed conflict against the Sri Lankan government and its military. Thousands of Sri Lankan troops repeatedly failed to dislodge the Tamil Tigers. Casualties were heavy among Sri Lankan police and military units, which often vented their personal frustrations on Tamil civilians with brutal massacres. These harsh measures caused thousands more Tamil to embrace the politics and policies of the LTTE.

INDIA'S INVOLVEMENT

India had quietly supported the Tamil terrorists until 1987, when the Indian government reversed its policies and tried to negotiate an end to hostilities between the Sri Lankan government and the Tamil separatists. But the LTTE refused to end its terrorist activities because the agreement didn't go far enough toward establishing a separate Tamil state.

Snubbed by the Tigers, India did a dramatic about-face and sent soldiers to Sri Lanka in 1987. They tried to root out the Tamil Tigers in LTTE-controlled areas, but the Indian attempt to break the battle-hardened LTTE failed disastrously. Indian forces fought LTTE guerrillas to a standstill in the Tamil city of Jaffna in battles that left hundreds dead and thousands of people wounded. By 1990 India had pulled out all of its troops.

(Above) In 1987 Sri Lankan president Junius Jayewardene *(left)* met with Indian prime minister Rajiv Gandhi *(right)* to discuss India's involvement in Sri Lanka's civil war. (Four years later, Gandhi was killed by an LTTE suicide bomber.) *(Right)* President Ranasinghe Premadasa, who succeeded Jayewardene, was also assassinated by an LTTE suicide bomber. Sri Lankan guards watch over his casket at his funeral.

The LTTE eventually added a new tactic to its strategic playbook—the use of female suicide bombers as political assassins. LTTE suicide bombers murdered Indian prime minister Rajiv Gandhi in May 1991 and Sri Lanka's Sinhalese president Ranasinghe Premadasa in 1993.

One of the most lethal attacks inside Sri Lanka was the massive truck bombing of the Central Bank in Colombo in January 1996. It was followed by an attack on the Colombo World Trade Center in October 1997. Both events killed hundreds of people.

Bloodied employees flee an LTTE bomb blast at the Central Bank of Colombo in 1996.

October 15, 1997

Most of Colombo residents were just waking up and not yet at work when a massive truck bomb, driven by an LTTE suicide bomber, exploded near two popular hotels and the Colombo World Trade Center. The massive bomb, believed to have contained more than one thousand pounds of explosives, sent glass and debris flying at furious speeds throughout the city's business district. Anyone in the immediate vicinity of the World Trade Center was obliterated by the powerful blast. Anyone in range of the wave of heat, energy, and shrapnel was seriously hurt.

But the suicide bombing in Colombo was just an opening salvo. Moments after the blast, LTTE terrorists rocked the area with two smaller explosions and a machine-gun assault. The Tigers were eager to make the point that they could strike anywhere in

Rescue workers tend to a wounded tourist after the Tamil Tiger attack on October 15, 1997.

the city, in any manner, and in bloody fashion. The gun battles between the terrorists and Sri Lanka's security forces lasted the entire day, paralyzing the city and preventing emergency rescue personnel from reaching ground zero of the World Trade Center. By the time sunset had descended on the Sri Lankan capital, twelve people had been killed and more than one hundred had been wounded.

A female LTTE guerrilla unit guards a crossing point into Tiger-held territory.

VELLUPILLAI PRABHAKARAN

Born in 1954 to a middle-class Tamil family, Vellupillai Prabhakaran was exposed to the struggle for Tamil separatism at a young age. An uncle was killed during the language riots of 1958, and other relatives beat the drum of militant resistance during his teens. By the 1970s, Prabhakaran had dropped out of high school and had formed his first separatist militant group. He later traveled to India, where he received training in guerrilla tactics and terrorist activities.

Prabhakaran held his 2002 press conference in an LTTE location secured by LTTE troops.

His part in the murder of Mayor Duriappah brought Prabhakaran to public attention, and he began to emerge as a powerful and charismatic separatist leader. He set up small combat units in the north that do not know about one another, so that one group's capture cannot endanger the larger group. His troops train hard in guerrilla warfare in the northern and eastern provinces, where Tamil are the majority.

Although Sri Lankan forces have long wanted to catch Prabhakaran, he has eluded them with disguises, by moving from house to house, and by surrounding himself with loyal bodyguards. During a 2002 press conference, the LTTE leader reemphasized the group's commitment to recognition of the Tamil as a distinct nationality, recognition of the northern and eastern provinces as their traditional homeland, and recognition of his people's right to determine their own future. ■

Prabhakaran's LTTE is believed to consist of some six thousand trained fighters. The elite band of suicide bombers, known as the Black Tigers, executes bloody terrorist attacks throughout the country. All LTTE terrorists, including Prabhakaran, carry a cyanide capsule to kill themselves rather than be captured and interrogated by Sri Lankan security forces. Many LTTE terrorists train at terrorist camps in the

The first round of the Norwegian-sponsored peace talks took place in Thailand. The Sri Lankan government's chief negotiator was G. L. Peiris *(left)*. His LTTE counterpart was Anton Balasingham *(right)*. Here, the two men arrive at the opening ceremonies.

Middle East and India. Many of the LTTE's men and women under arms—or on the LTTE payroll—are financed by heroin trafficking. The income earned from this illegal enterprise has brought millions of dollars into the LTTE war chest.

The long-standing conflict between the Sri Lankan government and the Tamil separatists has quieted in recent years, and a Norwegian-sponsored cease-fire went into effect in February 2002. At that time, in a show of mutual concessions, the LTTE agreed to the notion of regional autonomy instead of a separate Tamil state. The Sri Lankan government agreed to share power with the LTTE under a federal system. Meanwhile, the LTTE maintains a large terrorist army that can wage guerrilla warfare and suicide bombings at will.

EPILOGUE

THE IRA In May 2003, the October 2002 suspension of elections to the Stormont (the Northern Ireland assembly) was stretched to fall 2003. The British government cited the PIRA's refusal to completely rule out any future paramilitary operations as the reason for a further delay. Gerry Adams countered by saying that the PIRA would not engage in any activities that would undermine the peace process. Meanwhile, scattered episodes of paramilitary violence continued throughout the region.

THE ETA In March 2003, the Spanish supreme court upheld and made permanent the government's 2002 ban of Batasuna. In May 2003, under pressure from the Spanish government, the United States added Batasuna to its list of terrorist groups. The ETA was already on the U.S. list of foreign terrorist organizations.

THE PKK In March 2003, the European Court of Human Rights concluded that KADEK leader Abdullah Ocalan might not have received a fair trial. In May 2003, following the successful U.S.-led war against Iraq, Turkey expressed concerns that an independent Kurdish state may emerge in northern Iraq, where Turkey believes armed, hardcore KADEK supporters are in hiding.

THE LTTE Sri Lanka's peace process hit a snag in April 2003. The LTTE pulled out of the seventh round of peace talks because it was not invited to participate in talks between the Sri Lankan government and international donors. The LTTE assured the public that the cease-fire was still in place, however. Concerns linger that support for federal power sharing, which will require a change to Sri Lanka's constitution, will be difficult to build. Meanwhile, leaders of several Tamil opposition parties were assassinated. In May 2003, the parties accused the LTTE of using the cease-fire as a cover for the elimination and intimidation of their rivals before autonomy is in place. The LTTE denied the allegations. ∎

*Please note that the information contained in this book was current at the time of publication. To find sources for late-breaking news, please consult the websites listed on page 69.

TIMELINE

Northern Ireland	Basque lands
Sri Lanka	Kurdish lands

300 B.C. Kurdish kingdoms exist in mountains of southwestern Asia.

A.D. 432 Patrick arrives in Ireland to convert the Gaels to Christianity.

A.D. 824 Basques establish the kingdom of Pamplona in Spain.

1155 Pope Adrian IV grants English king Henry II lordship over Ireland.

1400s Ottoman Empire is established in southwestern Asia.

1514 Battle of Chaldiran puts nearly all Kurdish territory under Ottoman control.

1533 English king Henry VIII establishes Anglican Church.

1801 Act of Union, uniting England, Scotland, Wales, and Ireland goes into effect.

1802 Britain takes over Ceylon and makes it a colony.

1840s Irish potato famine takes place.

1895 Sabino Arana y Goiri establishes Basque Nationalist Party (PNV).

1914 World War I begins.

1916 Irish Republican Brotherhood organizes Easter Rising in Dublin.

1919 Sinn Féin establishes an independent Irish parliament in Dublin.

1921 Government of Ireland Act creates Irish Free State and Northern Ireland. Treaty of Sèvres sets forth creation of Kurdish state.

1923 Treaty of Lausanne divides up Kurdish lands.

1936 Basques support Popular Front in Spain in exchange for statute of autonomy.

1937 German air force bombs Basque town of Guernica.

1948 Britain grants Ceylon its independence.

1956 ▮▮▮▮▮▮▮▮▮▮▮▮▮▮▮▮▮▮▮▮▮▮▮▮▮

1959 Euskadi Ta Askatasuna (ETA) founded by
dissatisfied Basque students. Ceylon
prime minister SWRD Bandaranaike is assassinated.

1969 Provisional Irish Republican Army (PIRA) comes
into being.

1971 Janatha Vimukthi Peramuna (JVP) tries to seize
control of Ceylon.

1972 Bloody Sunday takes place in Londonderry,
Northern Ireland. Ceylon is renamed Sri Lanka.
Radical Tamil found the Liberation Tigers of
Tamil Eelam (LTTE).

1973 ETA assassinates Luis Carrero Blanco in Madrid, Spain.

1978 Abdullah Ocalan founds Partia Karkaren Kurdistan
(PKK) in Turkey. LTTE begins terrorist campaign
in many areas of Sri Lanka.

1970s– PIRA bomb attacks in Northern Ireland and Britain
1980s kill and injure thousands.

1987 PKK begins guerrilla war in Turkey. Indian government
sends troops to Sri Lanka to put down LTTE.

1989 Indian troops begin withdrawal from Sri Lanka,
having failed to suppress LTTE.

1990s ETA conducts a series of assassinations, kidnappings,
and bombings in Spain. LTTE suicide bombers kill
Sri Lankan and Indian politicians.

1997 PIRA cease-fire in Northern Ireland. Real IRA
(RIRA) comes into being in Northern Ireland.

1998 Good Friday Agreement wins majority support on
the Irish island.

1999 Abdullah Ocalan is apprehended in Africa. PKK
abandons the notion of Kurdish self-rule.

2000 Thousands of Spaniards march to end ETA bombings.

2002 Norway brokers a cease-fire between the Sri Lankan
government and the LTTE. PKK changes its name to
Congress for Freedom and Democracy in Kurdistan
(KADEK). British government suspends elections to
the Northern Ireland assembly.

SELECTED BIBLIOGRAPHY

Alexander, Yonah, and Dennis A. Pluchinsky, eds. *European Terrorism Today and Tomorrow.* McLean, VA: Brassey's US, Inc., 1992.

———. *Europe's Red Terrorists: The Fighting Communist Organizations.* London: Frank Cass and Company Ltd., 1992.

Bell, J. Bowyer. *IRA Tactics and Targets: An Analysis of Tactical Aspects of the Armed Struggle 1969–1989.* Dublin: Poolbeg, 1990.

Bishop, Patrick, and Mallie Eamonn. *The Provisional IRA.* London: Corgi Books, 1992.

Black, Eric. *Northern Ireland: Troubled Land.* Minneapolis, MN: Lerner Publications Company, 1998.

Bulloch, John, and Harvey Morris. *No Friends but the Mountains: The Tragic History of the Kurds.* Oxford: Oxford University Press, 1992.

Clark, Robert P. *The Basque Insurgents: ETA 1952–1980.* Madison, WI: University of Wisconsin Press, 1984.

Coogan, Tim Pat. *The IRA: A History.* Niwot, CO: Roberts Rinehart Publishers, 1993.

Dietl, Wilhelm. *Holy War.* New York: Macmillan, 1984.

Dobson, Christopher, and Ronald Payne. *The Never Ending: Terrorism in the 1980s.* New York: Facts on File, 1987.

Fuglerud, Oivind. *Life on the Outside: The Tamil Diaspora and Long Distance Nationalism.* London: Pluto Press, 1999.

Geraghty, Tony. *Who Dares Wins.* London: Warner Press, 1993.

Goren, Roberta. *The Soviet Union and Terrorism.* London: George Allen and Unwin, 1984.

Harnden, Toby. *'Bandit Country': The IRA and South Armagh.* Edinburgh: Hodder and Stoughton, 1999.

Izady, Mehrdad R. *The Kurds: A Concise Handbook.* New York: Crane Russak and Company, 1992.

Kurlansky, Mark. *The Basque History of the World.* New York: Penguin, 2001.

Laqueur, Walter. *Terrorism.* London: Weidenfeld and Nicolson, 1977.

MacDonald, Eileen. *Shoot the Women First.* New York: Random House, 1991.

McDowall, David. *A Modern History of the Kurds.* New York: I. B. Tauris and Company Ltd., 2001.

Nadelmann, Ethan A. *Cops across Borders.* University Park, PA: The Pennsylvania State University Press, 1993.

Randal, Jonathan C. *After Such Knowledge, What Forgiveness? My Encounters with Kurdistan.* Boulder, CO: Westview Press, 1999.

Rosie, George. *The Directory of International Terrorism.* Edinburgh: Mainstream Publishing Company, 1986.

Rotberg, Robert I., ed. *Creating Peace in Sri Lanka: Civil War and Reconciliation.* Washington, D.C.: Brookings Institute, 1999.

Sterling, Claire. *The Terror Network.* New York: Berkeley Books, 1981.

Tambiah, Stanley Jeyaraja. *Sri Lanka: Ethnic Fratricide and the Dismantling of Democracy.* Chicago: University of Chicago Press, 1991.

Urban, Mark. *Big Boys' Rules: The Secret Struggles against the IRA.* London: Faber and Faber Ltd., 1992.

Woodworth, Paddy. *Dirty Wars, Clean Hands: ETA, the GAL, and Spanish Democracy.* Cork, Ireland: Cork University Press, 2001.

Zwier, Lawrence, J. *Sri Lanka: War-Torn Island.* Minneapolis, MN: Lerner Publications Company, 1998.

FURTHER READING AND WEBSITES

Books

Black, Eric. *Northern Ireland: Troubled Land*. Minneapolis, MN: Lerner Publications Company, 1998.

Bodnarchuk, Kari. *Kurdistan: Region Under Siege*. Minneapolis, MN: Lerner Publications Company, 2000.

Currie, Stephen. *Terrorists and Terrorist Groups*. San Diego, CA: Lucent Books, 2002.

Fridell, Ron. *Terrorism: Political Violence at Home and Abroad*. Berkely Heights, NJ: Enslow Publishers, 2001.

Meltzer, Milton. *The Day the Sky Fell: A History of Terrorism*. New York: Random Library, 2002.

Sarat, Austin. *Terrorism*. Philadelphia: Chelsea House Publications, 1998.

Taylor, Robert. *The History of Terrorism*. San Diego, CA: Lucent Books, 2002.

Wagner, Heather Lehr. *The IRA and England*. Philadelphia: Chelsea House Publications, 2002.

Zwier, Lawrence J. *Sri Lanka: War-Torn Island*. Minneapolis, MN: Lerner Publications Company, 1998.

Websites

BBC News: World Edition
<http://news.bbc.co.uk>
This website offers extensive international coverage of news and world events.

CNN.com
<http://www.cnn.com>
This site provides late-breaking news about all the conflicts discussed in this book.

Economist.com
<http://www.economist.com>
Regularly updated, this online version of *The Economist* magazine offers up-to-date economic information, as well as commentary on how terrorist activities affect local and world economies.

The New York Times on the Web
<http://www.nytimes.com>
This online version of the newspaper offers both up-to-date and archived articles on the major terrorist groups.

The Terrorism Research Center
<http://www.terrorism.com>
In addition to its historic information on terrorist groups, this site also provides antiterrorist information and links to other useful sites.

Time Online Edition
<http://www.time.com/time>
This online version of the magazine can be searched by specific continents as well as in general.

U.S. Department of State Counterterrorism Office
<http://www.state.gov/s/ct>
The U.S. government maintains this site, which offers information on historic and active terrorist groups.

INDEX

ABOUT THE AUTHOR

Samuel M. Katz is an expert in the field of international terrorism and counterterrorism, military special operations, and law enforcement. He has written more than twenty books and dozens of articles on these subjects, as well as creating documentaries and giving lectures. Mr. Katz also serves as editor in chief of *Special Ops*, a magazine dedicated to the discussion of special operations around the world, and observes counterterrorism units in action in Europe and the Middle East. The Terrorist Dossiers series is his first foray into the field of juvenile nonfiction.

PHOTO ACKNOWLEDGMENTS

All attempts have been made to contact the copyright holders(s) of the images in this book. If your image appears without proper credit, please contact Lerner Publishing Group.

The images in this book are used with the permission of: © Samuel M. Katz, pp. 5, 33 (both); © North Wind Picture Archives, p. 9; © Hulton-Deutsch Collection/CORBIS, p. 10; Imperial War Museum, p. 12; © Express News/Hulton/Archive, p. 13; © Ed Kashi/CORBIS, p. 14; © Bettman/CORBIS, pp. 15, 39, 55; © David Robinson/CORBIS, p. 17; © Francis Dias/CORBIS SYGMA, p. 18; © Reuters/Paul Hackett/Getty Images, p. 19; © Reuters NewMedia, Inc./CORBIS, pp. 20, 21, 62 (bottom), 63; Basque Library, University of Nevada, Reno, pp. 23, 26; © Mark Kurlansky, p. 24; Sabino Arana Foundation, Bilboa, p. 25; © Hulton/Archive, pp. 27, 29, 56; © Nik Wheeler/CORBIS, p. 30; © AFP/CORBIS, pp. 31, 35, 49; © CORBIS/SYGMA, pp. 32, 45; © The Art Archive/Bodleian Library Oxford/The Bodleian Library, p. 38; © CORBIS, p. 40; © Popperfoto, p. 43; © The Kurdish Library, pp. 44, 46; © M. Attar/CORBIS SYGMA, p. 47; © Ed Kashi, p. 48; © Caroline Penn/CORBIS, p. 50; © AP/Wide World Photos/ HURRIYET, p. 51; The Illustrated London News Picture Library, p. 53; © AP/Wide World Photos, pp. 54, 60 (left); © Dinodia Photo Library, pp. 57, 58 (bottom), 59; © Panos Pictures, p. 58 (top); © BALDEV/CORBIS SYGMA, p. 60 (right); © Reuters/ Anuruddha Lokuhapuarachchi, p. 61; © Reuters/Anuruddha Lokuhapuarachchi/Getty Images, p. 62 (top); © Reuters/Jason Reed/Getty Images, p. 64. Map on page 37 by Laura Westlund. Cover © Lewis Alan/CORBIS SYGMA.